THE AUGSBURG CONFESSION

LECTOR HOUSE PUBLIC DOMAIN WORKS

THE AUGSBURG CONFESSION

PHILIP MELANCHTHON,
FRIEDRICH BENTE,
WILLIAM HERMAN THEODORE DAU

ISBN: 978-93-5420-149-3

Published: -

© 2020
LECTOR HOUSE LLP

LECTOR HOUSE

LECTOR HOUSE LLP
E-MAIL: lectorpublishing@gmail.com

THE AUGSBURG CONFESSION

THE CONFESSION OF FAITH:
WHICH WAS SUBMITTED TO HIS IMPERIAL MAJESTY CHARLES V AT THE DIET OF AUGSBURG IN THE YEAR 1530

BY

PHILIP MELANCHTHON

TRANSLATED BY
F. BENTE AND W. H. T. DAU

PREFACE TO THE EMPEROR CHARLES V.

Most Invincible Emperor, Caesar Augustus, Most Clement Lord: Inasmuch as Your Imperial Majesty has summoned a Diet of the Empire here at Augsburg to deliberate concerning measures against the Turk, that most atrocious, hereditary, and ancient enemy of the Christian name and religion, in what way, namely, effectually to withstand his furor and assaults by strong and lasting military provision; and then also concerning dissensions in the matter of our holy religion and Christian Faith, that in this matter of religion the opinions and judgments of the parties might be heard in each other's presence; and considered and weighed among ourselves in mutual charity, leniency, and kindness, in order that, after the removal and correction of such things as have been treated and understood in a different manner in the writings on either side, these matters may be settled and brought back to one simple truth and Christian concord, that for the future one pure and true religion may be embraced and maintained by us, that as we all are under one Christ and do battle under Him, so we may be able also to live in unity and concord in the one Christian Church.

And inasmuch as we, the undersigned Elector and Princes, with others joined with us, have been called to the aforesaid Diet the same as the other Electors, Princes, and Estates, in obedient compliance with the Imperial mandate, we have promptly come to Augsburg, and — what we do not mean to say as boasting — we were among the first to be here.

Accordingly, since even here at Augsburg at the very beginning of the Diet, Your Imperial Majesty caused to be proposed to the Electors, Princes, and other Estates of the Empire, amongst other things, that the several Estates of the Empire, on the strength of the Imperial edict, should set forth and submit their opinions and judgments in the German and the Latin language, and since on the ensuing Wednesday, answer was given to Your Imperial Majesty, after due deliberation, that we would submit the Articles of our Confession for our side on next Wednesday, therefore, in obedience to Your Imperial Majesty's wishes, we offer, in this matter of religion, the Confession of our preachers and of ourselves, showing what manner of doctrine from the Holy Scriptures and the pure Word of God has been up to this time set forth in our lands, dukedoms, dominions, and cities, and taught in our churches.

And if the other Electors, Princes, and Estates of the Empire will, according to the said Imperial proposition, present similar writings, to wit, in Latin and German, giving their opinions in this matter of religion, we, with the Princes and friends aforesaid, here before Your Imperial Majesty, our most clement Lord are prepared to confer amicably concerning all possible ways and means, in order that we may come together, as far as this may be honorably done, and, the matter between us on both sides being peacefully discussed without offensive strife, the dissension, by God's help, may be done away and brought back to one true accordant religion; for as we all are under one Christ and do battle under Him, we ought to confess the one Christ, after the tenor of Your Imperial Majesty's edict, and everything ought to be conducted according to the truth of God; and this it is what, with most fervent prayers, we entreat of God.

However, as regards the rest of the Electors, Princes, and Estates, who constitute the other part, if no progress should be made, nor some result be attained by this treatment of the cause of religion after the manner in which Your Imperial Majesty has wisely held that it should be dealt with and treated namely, by such mutual presentation of writings and calm conferring together among ourselves, we at least leave with you a clear testimony, that we here in no wise are holding back from anything that could bring about Christian concord,—such as could be effected with God and a good conscience,—as also Your Imperial Majesty and, next, the other Electors and Estates of the Empire, and all who are moved by sincere love and zeal for religion, and who will give an impartial hearing to this matter, will graciously deign to take notice and to understand this from this Confession of ours and of our associates.

Your Imperial Majesty also, not only once but often, graciously signified to the Electors Princes, and Estates of the Empire, and at the Diet of Spires held A. D. 1526, according to the form of Your Imperial instruction and commission given and prescribed, caused it to be stated and publicly proclaimed that Your Majesty, in dealing with this matter of religion, for certain reasons which were alleged in Your Majesty's name, was not willing to decide and could not determine anything, but that Your Majesty would diligently use Your Majesty's office with the Roman Pontiff for the convening of a General Council. The same matter was thus publicly set forth at greater length a year ago at the last Diet which met at Spires. There Your Imperial Majesty, through His Highness Ferdinand, King of Bohemia and Hungary, our friend and clement Lord, as well as through the Orator and Imperial Commissioners caused this, among other things, to be submitted: that Your Imperial Majesty had taken notice of; and pondered, the resolution of Your Majesty's Representative in the Empire, and of the President and Imperial Counselors, and the Legates from other Estates convened at Ratisbon, concerning the calling of a Council, and that your Imperial Majesty also judged it to be expedient to convene a Council; and that Your Imperial Majesty did not doubt the Roman Pontiff could be induced to hold a General Council, because the matters to be adjusted between Your Imperial Majesty and the Roman Pontiff were nearing agreement and Christian reconciliation; therefore Your Imperial Majesty himself signified that he would endeavor to secure the said Chief Pontiff's consent for convening, together with your Imperial Majesty such General Council, to be published as soon as possible by letters that were to be sent out.

If the outcome, therefore, should be such that the differences between us and the other parties in the matter of religion should not be amicably and in charity settled, then here, before Your Imperial Majesty we make the offer in all obedience, in addition to what we have already done, that we will all appear and defend our cause in such a general, free Christian Council, for the convening of which there has always been accordant action and agreement of votes in all the Imperial Diets held during Your Majesty's reign, on the part of the Electors, Princes, and other Estates of the Empire. To the assembly of this General Council, and at the same time to Your Imperial Majesty, we have, even before this, in due manner and form of law, addressed ourselves and made appeal in this matter, by far the greatest and gravest. To this appeal, both to Your Imperial Majesty and to a Council, we still adhere; neither do we intend nor would it be possible for us, to relinquish it by this or any other document, unless the matter between us and the other side, according to the tenor of the latest Imperial citation should be amicably and charitably settled, allayed, and brought to Christian concord; and regarding this we even here solemnly and publicly testify.

CONTENTS

CONTENTS

ARTICLES IN WHICH ARE REVIEWED THE ABUSES WHICH HAVE BEEN CORRECTED.

ARTICLE I.
OF GOD.

Our Churches, with common consent, do teach that the decree of the Council of Nicaea concerning the Unity of the Divine Essence and concerning the Three Persons, is true and to be believed without any doubting; that is to say, there is one Divine Essence which is called and which is God: eternal, without body, without parts, of infinite power, wisdom, and goodness, the Maker and Preserver of all things, visible and invisible; and yet there are three Persons, of the same essence and power, who also are coeternal, the Father the Son, and the Holy Ghost. And the term "person" they use as the Fathers have used it, to signify, not a part or quality in another, but that which subsists of itself.

They condemn all heresies which have sprung up against this article, as the Manichaeans, who assumed two principles, one Good and the other Evil—also the Valentinians, Arians, Eunomians, Mohammedans, and all such. They condemn also the Samosatenes, old and new, who, contending that there is but one Person, sophistically and impiously argue that the Word and the Holy Ghost are not distinct Persons, but that "Word" signifies a spoken word, and "Spirit" signifies motion created in things.

ARTICLE II.
OF ORIGINAL SIN.

Also they teach that since the fall of Adam all men begotten in the natural way are born with sin, that is, without the fear of God, without trust in God, and with concupiscence; and that this disease, or vice of origin, is truly sin, even now condemning and bringing eternal death upon those not born again through Baptism and the Holy Ghost.

They Condemn the Pelagians and others who deny that original depravity is sin, and who, to obscure the glory of Christ's merit and benefits, argue that man can be justified before God by his own strength and reason.

ARTICLE III.

OF THE SON OF GOD.

Also they teach that the Word, that is, the Son of God, did assume the human nature in the womb of the blessed Virgin Mary, so that there are two natures, the divine and the human, inseparably enjoined in one Person, one Christ, true God and true man, who was born of the Virgin Mary, truly suffered, was crucified, dead, and buried, that He might reconcile the Father unto us, and be a sacrifice, not only for original guilt, but also for all actual sins of men.

He also descended into hell, and truly rose again the third day; afterward He ascended into heaven that He might sit on the right hand of the Father, and forever reign and have dominion over all creatures, and sanctify them that believe in Him, by sending the Holy Ghost into their hearts, to rule, comfort, and quicken them, and to defend them against the devil and the power of sin.

The same Christ shall openly come again to judge the quick and the dead, etc., according to the Apostles' Creed.

ARTICLE IV.
OF JUSTIFICATION.

Also they teach that men cannot be justified before God by their own strength, merits, or works, but are freely justified for Christ's sake, through faith, when they believe that they are received into favor, and that their sins are forgiven for Christ's sake, who, by His death, has made satisfaction for our sins. This faith God imputes for righteousness in His sight. Rom. 3 and 4.

ARTICLE V.
OF THE MINISTRY.

That we may obtain this faith, the Ministry of Teaching the Gospel and administering the Sacraments was instituted. For through the Word and Sacraments, as through instruments, the Holy Ghost is given, who works faith; where and when it pleases God, in them that hear the Gospel, to wit, that God, not for our own merits, but for Christ's sake, justifies those who believe that they are received into grace for Christ's sake.

They condemn the Anabaptists and others who think that the Holy Ghost comes to men without the external Word, through their own preparations and works.

ARTICLE VI.
OF NEW OBEDIENCE.

Also they teach that this faith is bound to bring forth good fruits, and that it is necessary to do good works commanded by God, because of God's will, but that we should not rely on those works to merit justification before God. For remission of sins and justification is apprehended by faith, as also the voice of Christ attests: When ye shall have done all these things, say: We are unprofitable servants. Luke 17, 10. The same is also taught by the Fathers. For Ambrose says: It is ordained of God that he who believes in Christ is saved, freely receiving remission of sins, without works, by faith alone.

ARTICLE VII.
OF THE CHURCH.

Also they teach that one holy Church is to continue forever. The Church is the congregation of saints, in which the Gospel is rightly taught and the Sacraments are rightly administered.

And to the true unity of the Church it is enough to agree concerning the doctrine of the Gospel and the administration of the Sacraments. Nor is it necessary that human traditions, that is, rites or ceremonies, instituted by men, should be everywhere alike. As Paul says: One faith, one Baptism, one God and Father of all, etc. Eph. 4, 5. 6.

ARTICLE VIII.
WHAT THE CHURCH IS.

Although the Church properly is the congregation of saints and true believers, nevertheless, since in this life many hypocrites and evil persons are mingled therewith, it is lawful to use Sacraments administered by evil men, according to the saying of Christ: The Scribes and the Pharisees sit in Moses' seat, etc. Matt. 23, 2. Both the Sacraments and Word are effectual by reason of the institution and commandment of Christ, notwithstanding they be administered by evil men.

They condemn the Donatists, and such like, who denied it to be lawful to use the ministry of evil men in the Church, and who thought the ministry of evil men to be unprofitable and of none effect.

ARTICLE IX.

OF BAPTISM.

Of Baptism they teach that it is necessary to salvation, and that through Baptism is offered the grace of God, and that children are to be baptized who, being offered to God through Baptism are received into God's grace.

They condemn the Anabaptists, who reject the baptism of children, and say that children are saved without Baptism.

ARTICLE X.
OF THE LORD'S SUPPER.

Of the Supper of the Lord they teach that the Body and Blood of Christ are truly present, and are distributed to those who eat the Supper of the Lord; and they reject those that teach otherwise.

ARTICLE XI.
OF CONFESSION.

Of Confession they teach that Private Absolution ought to be retained in the churches, although in confession an enumeration of all sins is not necessary. For it is impossible according to the Psalm: Who can understand his errors? Ps. 19, 12.

ARTICLE XII.
OF REPENTANCE.

Of Repentance they teach that for those who have fallen after Baptism there is remission of sins whenever they are converted and that the Church ought to impart absolution to those thus returning to repentance. Now, repentance consists properly of these two parts: One is contrition, that is, terrors smiting the conscience through the knowledge of sin; the other is faith, which is born of the Gospel, or of absolution, and believes that for Christ's sake, sins are forgiven, comforts the conscience, and delivers it from terrors. Then good works are bound to follow, which are the fruits of repentance.

They condemn the Anabaptists, who deny that those once justified can lose the Holy Ghost. Also those who contend that some may attain to such perfection in this life that they cannot sin.

The Novatians also are condemned, who would not absolve such as had fallen after Baptism, though they returned to repentance.

They also are rejected who do not teach that remission of sins comes through faith but command us to merit grace through satisfactions of our own.

ARTICLE XIII.
OF THE USE OF THE SACRAMENTS.

Of the Use of the Sacraments they teach that the Sacraments were ordained, not only to be marks of profession among men, but rather to be signs and testimonies of the will of God toward us, instituted to awaken and confirm faith in those who use them. Wherefore we must so use the Sacraments that faith be added to believe the promises which are offered and set forth through the Sacraments.

They therefore condemn those who teach that the Sacraments justify by the outward act, and who do not teach that, in the use of the Sacraments, faith which believes that sins are forgiven, is required.

ARTICLE XIV.
OF ECCLESIASTICAL ORDER.

Of Ecclesiastical Order they teach that no one should publicly teach in the Church or administer the Sacraments unless he be regularly called.

ARTICLE XV.
OF ECCLESIASTICAL USAGES.

Of Usages in the Church they teach that those ought to be observed which may be observed without sin, and which are profitable unto tranquillity and good order in the Church, as particular holy-days, festivals, and the like.

Nevertheless, concerning such things men are admonished that consciences are not to be burdened, as though such observance was necessary to salvation.

They are admonished also that human traditions instituted to propitiate God, to merit grace, and to make satisfaction for sins, are opposed to the Gospel and the doctrine of faith. Wherefore vows and traditions concerning meats and days, etc., instituted to merit grace and to make satisfaction for sins, are useless and contrary to the Gospel.

ARTICLE XVI.
OF CIVIL AFFAIRS.

Of Civil Affairs they teach that lawful civil ordinances are good works of God, and that it is right for Christians to bear civil office, to sit as judges, to judge matters by the Imperial and other existing laws, to award just punishments, to engage in just wars, to serve as soldiers, to make legal contracts, to hold property, to make oath when required by the magistrates, to marry a wife, to be given in marriage.

They condemn the Anabaptists who forbid these civil offices to Christians.

They condemn also those who do not place evangelical perfection in the fear of God and in faith, but in forsaking civil offices, for the Gospel teaches an eternal righteousness of the heart. Meanwhile, it does not destroy the State or the family, but very much requires that they be preserved as ordinances of God, and that charity be practiced in such ordinances. Therefore, Christians are necessarily bound to obey their own magistrates and laws save only when commanded to sin; for then they ought to obey God rather than men. Acts 5, 29.

ARTICLE XVII.

OF CHRIST'S RETURN TO JUDGMENT.

Also they teach that at the Consummation of the World Christ will appear for judgment and will raise up all the dead; He will give to the godly and elect eternal life and everlasting joys, but ungodly men and the devils He will condemn to be tormented without end.

They condemn the Anabaptists, who think that there will be an end to the punishments of condemned men and devils.

They condemn also others who are now spreading certain Jewish opinions, that before the resurrection of the dead the godly shall take possession of the kingdom of the world, the ungodly being everywhere suppressed.

ARTICLE XVIII.

OF FREE WILL.

Of Free Will they teach that man's will has some liberty to choose civil righteousness, and to work things subject to reason. But it has no power, without the Holy Ghost, to work the righteousness of God, that is, spiritual righteousness; since the natural man receiveth not the things of the Spirit of God, 1 Cor. 2,14; but this righteousness is wrought in the heart when the Holy Ghost is received through the Word. These things are said in as many words by Augustine in his Hypognosticon, Book III: We grant that all men have a free will, free, inasmuch as it has the judgment of reason; not that it is thereby capable, without God, either to begin, or, at least, to complete aught in things pertaining to God, but only in works of this life, whether good or evil. "Good" I call those works which spring from the good in nature, such as, willing to labor in the field, to eat and drink, to have a friend, to clothe oneself, to build a house, to marry a wife, to raise cattle, to learn divers useful arts, or whatsoever good pertains to this life. For all of these things are not without dependence on the providence of God; yea, of Him and through Him they are and have their being. "Evil" I call such works as willing to worship an idol, to commit murder, etc.

They condemn the Pelagians and others, who teach that without the Holy Ghost, by the power of nature alone, we are able to love God above all things; also to do the commandments of God as touching "the substance of the act." For, although nature is able in a manner to do the outward work, (for it is able to keep the hands from theft and murder,) yet it cannot produce the inward motions, such as the fear of God, trust in God, chastity, patience, etc.

ARTICLE XIX.

OF THE CAUSE OF SIN.

Of the Cause of Sin they teach that, although God does create and preserve nature, yet the cause of sin is the will of the wicked, that is, of the devil and ungodly men; which will, unaided of God, turns itself from God, as Christ says John 8, 44: When he speaketh a lie, he speaketh of his own.

ARTICLE XX.
OF GOOD WORKS.

Our teachers are falsely accused of forbidding good Works. For their published writings on the Ten Commandments, and others of like import, bear witness that they have taught to good purpose concerning all estates and duties of life, as to what estates of life and what works in every calling be pleasing to God. Concerning these things preachers heretofore taught but little, and urged only childish and needless works, as particular holy-days, particular fasts, brotherhoods, pilgrimages, services in honor of saints, the use of rosaries, monasticism, and such like. Since our adversaries have been admonished of these things, they are now unlearning them, and do not preach these unprofitable works as heretofore. Besides, they begin to mention faith, of which there was heretofore marvelous silence. They teach that we are justified not by works only, but they conjoin faith and works, and say that we are justified by faith and works. This doctrine is more tolerable than the former one, and can afford more consolation than their old doctrine.

Forasmuch, therefore, as the doctrine concerning faith, which ought to be the chief one in the Church, has lain so long unknown, as all must needs grant that there was the deepest silence in their sermons concerning the righteousness of faith, while only the doctrine of works was treated in the churches, our teachers have instructed the churches concerning faith as follows: —

First, that our works cannot reconcile God or merit forgiveness of sins, grace, and justification, but that we obtain this only by faith when we believe that we are received into favor for Christs sake, who alone has been set forth the Mediator and Propitiation, 1 Tim. 2, 6, in order that the Father may be reconciled through Him. Whoever, therefore, trusts that by works he merits grace, despises the merit and grace of Christ, and seeks a way to God without Christ, by human strength, although Christ has said of Himself: I am the Way, the Truth, and the Life. John 14, 6.

This doctrine concerning faith is everywhere treated by Paul, Eph. 2, 8: By grace are ye saved through faith; and that not of yourselves; it is the gift of God, not of works, etc.

And lest any one should craftily say that a new interpretation of Paul has been devised by us, this entire matter is supported by the testimonies of the Fathers. For Augustine, in many volumes, defends grace and the righteousness of faith, over against the merits of works. And Ambrose, in his De Vocatione Gentium, and elsewhere, teaches to like effect. For in his De Vocatione Gentium he says as follows: Redemption by the blood of Christ would become of little value, neither would the preeminence of man's works be superseded by the mercy of God, if justification, which is wrought through grace, were due to the merits going before, so as to be, not the free gift of a donor, but the reward due to the laborer.

But, although this doctrine is despised by the inexperienced, nevertheless God-fearing and anxious consciences find by experience that it brings the greatest consolation, because consciences cannot be set at rest through any works, but only by faith, when they take the sure ground that for Christ's sake they have a reconciled God. As Paul teaches Rom. 5, 1: Being justified by faith, we have peace with God. This whole doctrine is to be referred to that conflict of the terrified conscience, neither can it be understood apart from that conflict. Therefore inexperienced and profane men judge ill concerning this matter, who dream that Christian righteousness is nothing but civil and philosophical righteousness.

Heretofore consciences were plagued with the doctrine of works, they did not hear the consolation from the Gospel. Some persons were driven by conscience into the desert, into monasteries hoping there to merit grace by a monastic life. Some also devised other works whereby to merit grace and make satisfaction for sins. Hence there was very great need to treat of, and renew, this doctrine of faith in Christ, to the end that anxious consciences should not be without consolation but that they might know that grace and forgiveness of sins and justification are apprehended by faith in Christ.

Men are also admonished that here the term "faith" does not signify merely the knowledge of the history, such as is in the ungodly and in the devil, but signifies a faith which believes, not merely the history, but also the effect of the history—namely, this Article: the forgiveness of sins, to wit, that we have grace, righteousness, and forgiveness of sins through Christ.

Now he that knows that he has a Father gracious to him through Christ, truly knows God; he knows also that God cares for him, and calls upon God; in a word, he is not without God, as the heathen. For devils and the ungodly are not able to believe this Article: the forgiveness of sins. Hence, they hate God as an enemy, call not upon Him, and expect no good from Him. Augustine also admonishes his readers concerning the word "faith," and teaches that the term "faith" is accepted in the Scriptures not for knowledge such as is in the ungodly but for confidence which consoles and encourages the terrified mind.

Furthermore, it is taught on our part that it is necessary to do good works, not that we should trust to merit grace by them, but because it is the will of God. It is only by faith that forgiveness of sins is apprehended, and that, for nothing. And because through faith the Holy Ghost is received, hearts are renewed and endowed with new affections, so as to be able to bring forth good works. For Ambrose says: Faith is the mother of a good will and right doing. For man's powers without the Holy Ghost are full of ungodly affections, and are too weak to do works which are good in God's sight. Besides, they are in the power of the devil who impels men to divers sins, to ungodly opinions, to open crimes. This we may see in the philosophers, who, although they endeavored to live an honest life could not succeed, but were defiled with many open crimes. Such is the feebleness of man when he is without faith and without the Holy Ghost, and governs himself only by human strength.

Hence it may be readily seen that this doctrine is not to be charged with prohibiting good works, but rather the more to be commended, because it shows how we are enabled to do good works. For without faith human nature can in no wise do the works of the First or of the Second Commandment. Without faith it does not call upon God, nor expect anything from God, nor bear the cross, but seeks, and trusts in, man's help. And thus, when there is no faith and trust in God all manner of lusts and human devices rule in the heart. Wherefore Christ said, John 16,6: Without Me ye can do nothing; and the Church sings:

> Lacking Thy divine favor,
> There is nothing found in man,
> Naught in him is harmless.

ARTICLE XXI.

OF THE WORSHIP OF THE SAINTS.

Of the Worship of Saints they teach that the memory of saints may be set before us, that we may follow their faith and good works, according to our calling, as the Emperor may follow the example of David in making war to drive away the Turk from his country; For both are kings. But the Scripture teaches not the invocation of saints or to ask help of saints, since it sets before us the one Christ as the Mediator, Propitiation, High Priest, and Intercessor. He is to be prayed to, and has promised that He will hear our prayer; and this worship He approves above all, to wit, that in all afflictions He be called upon, 1 John 2, 1: If any man sin, we have an Advocate with the Father, etc.

This is about the Sum of our Doctrine, in which, as can be seen, there is nothing that varies from the Scriptures, or from the Church Catholic, or from the Church of Rome as known from its writers. This being the case, they judge harshly who insist that our teachers be regarded as heretics. There is, however, disagreement on certain Abuses, which have crept into the Church without rightful authority. And even in these, if there were some difference, there should be proper lenity on the part of bishops to bear with us by reason of the Confession which we have now reviewed; because even the Canons are not so severe as to demand the same rites everywhere, neither, at any time, have the rites of all churches been the same; although, among us, in large part, the ancient rites are diligently observed. For it is a false and malicious charge that all the ceremonies, all the things instituted of old, are abolished in our churches. But it has been a common complaint that some abuses were connected with the ordinary rites. These, inasmuch as they could not be approved with a good conscience, have been to some extent corrected.

ARTICLES IN WHICH ARE REVIEWED THE ABUSES WHICH HAVE BEEN CORRECTED.

Inasmuch, then, as our churches dissent in no article of the faith from the Church Catholic, but only omit some abuses which are new, and which have been erroneously accepted by the corruption of the times, contrary to the intent of the Canons, we pray that Your Imperial Majesty would graciously hear both what has been changed, and what were the reasons why the people were not compelled to observe those abuses against their conscience. Nor should Your Imperial Majesty believe those who, in order to excite the hatred of men against our part, disseminate strange slanders among the people. Having thus excited the minds of good men, they have first given occasion to this controversy, and now endeavor, by the same arts, to increase the discord. For Your Imperial Majesty will undoubtedly find that the form of doctrine and of ceremonies with us is not so intolerable as these ungodly and malicious men represent. Besides, the truth cannot be gathered from common rumors or the revilings of enemies. But it can readily be judged that nothing would serve better to maintain the dignity of ceremonies, and to nourish reverence and pious devotion among the people than if the ceremonies were observed rightly in the churches.

ARTICLE XXII.

OF BOTH KINDS IN THE SACRAMENT.

To the laity are given Both Kinds in the Sacrament of the Lord's Supper, because this usage has the commandment of the Lord in Matt. 26, 27: Drink ye all of it, where Christ has manifestly commanded concerning the cup that all should drink.

And lest any man should craftily say that this refers only to priests, Paul in 1 Cor. 11,27 recites an example from which it appears that the whole congregation did use both kinds. And this usage has long remained in the Church, nor is it known when, or by whose authority, it was changed; although Cardinal Cusanus mentions the time when it was approved. Cyprian in some places testifies that the blood was given to the people. The same is testified by Jerome, who says: The priests administer the Eucharist, and distribute the blood of Christ to the people. Indeed, Pope Gelasius commands that the Sacrament be not divided (dist. II., De Consecratione, cap. Comperimus). Only custom, not so ancient, has it otherwise. But it is evident that any custom introduced against the commandments of God is not to be allowed, as the Canons witness (dist. III., cap. Veritate, and the following chapters). But this custom has been received, not only against the Scripture, but also against the old Canons and the example of the Church. Therefore, if any preferred to use both kinds of the Sacrament, they ought not to have been compelled with offense to their consciences to do otherwise. And because the division of the Sacrament does not agree with the ordinance of Christ, we are accustomed to omit the procession, which hitherto has been in use.

ARTICLE XXIII.

OF THE MARRIAGE OF PRIESTS.

There has been common complaint concerning the examples of priests who were not chaste. For that reason also Pope Pius is reported to have said that there were certain causes why marriage was taken away from priests, but that there were far weightier ones why it ought to be given back; for so Platina writes. Since, therefore, our priests were desirous to avoid these open scandals, they married wives, and taught that it was lawful for them to contract matrimony. First, because Paul says, 1 Cor. 7, 2. 9: To avoid fornication, let every man have his own wife. Also: It is better to marry than to burn. Secondly Christ says, Matt. 19,11: All men cannot receive this saying, where He teaches that not all men are fit to lead a single life; for God created man for procreation, Gen. 1, 28. Nor is it in man's power, without a singular gift and work of God, to alter this creation. [For it is manifest, and many have confessed that no good, honest, chaste life, no Christian, sincere, upright conduct has resulted (from the attempt), but a horrible, fearful unrest and torment of conscience has been felt by many until the end.] Therefore, those who are not fit to lead a single life ought to contract matrimony. For no man's law, no vow, can annul the commandment and ordinance of God. For these reasons the priests teach that it is lawful for them to marry wives.

It is also evident that in the ancient Church priests were married men. For Paul says, 1 Tim. 3, 2, that a bishop should be chosen who is the husband of one wife. And in Germany, four hundred years ago for the first time, the priests were violently compelled to lead a single life, who indeed offered such resistance that the Archbishop of Mayence, when about to publish the Pope's decree concerning this matter, was almost killed in the tumult raised by the enraged priests. And so harsh was the dealing in the matter that not only were marriages forbidden for the future, but also existing marriages were torn asunder, contrary to all laws, divine and human, contrary even to the Canons themselves, made not only by the Popes, but by most celebrated Synods. [Moreover, many God-fearing and intelligent people in high station are known frequently to have expressed misgivings that such enforced celibacy and depriving men of marriage (which God Himself has instituted and left free to men) has never produced any good results, but has brought on many great and evil vices and much iniquity.]

Seeing also that, as the world is aging, man's nature is gradually growing weaker, it is well to guard that no more vices steal into Germany.

Furthermore, God ordained marriage to be a help against human infirmity.

The Canons themselves say that the old rigor ought now and then, in the latter times, to be relaxed because of the weakness of men; which it is to be wished were done also in this matter. And it is to be expected that the churches shall at some time lack pastors if marriage is any longer forbidden.

But while the commandment of God is in force, while the custom of the Church is well known, while impure celibacy causes many scandals, adulteries, and other crimes deserving the punishments of just magistrates, yet it is a marvelous thing that in nothing is more cruelty exercised than against the marriage of priests. God has given commandment to honor marriage. By the laws of all well-ordered commonwealths, even among the heathen, marriage is most highly honored. But now men, and that, priests, are cruelly put to death, contrary to the intent of the Canons, for no other cause than marriage. Paul, in 1 Tim. 4,3, calls that a doctrine of devils which forbids marriage. This may now be readily understood when the law against marriage is maintained by such penalties.

But as no law of man can annul the commandment of God, so neither can it be done by any vow. Accordingly, Cyprian also advises that women who do not keep the chastity they have promised should marry. His words are these (Book I, Epistle XI): But if they be unwilling or unable to persevere, it is better for them to marry than to fall into the fire by their lusts; they should certainly give no offense to their brethren and sisters.

And even the Canons show some leniency toward those who have taken vows before the proper age, as heretofore has generally been the ease.

ARTICLE XXIV.

OF THE MASS.

Falsely are our churches accused of abolishing the Mass; for the Mass is retained among us, and celebrated with the highest reverence. Nearly all the usual ceremonies are also preserved, save that the parts sung in Latin are interspersed here and there with German hymns, which have been added to teach the people. For ceremonies are needed to this end alone that the unlearned be taught [what they need to know of Christ]. And not only has Paul commanded to use in the church a language understood by the people 1 Cor. 14,2. 9, but it has also been so ordained by man's law. The people are accustomed to partake of the Sacrament together, if any be fit for it, and this also increases the reverence and devotion of public worship. For none are admitted except they be first examined. The people are also advised concerning the dignity and use of the Sacrament, how great consolation it brings anxious consciences, that they may learn to believe God, and to expect and ask of Him all that is good. [In this connection they are also instructed regarding other and false teachings on the Sacrament.] This worship pleases God; such use of the Sacrament nourishes true devotion toward God. It does not, therefore, appear that the Mass is more devoutly celebrated among our adversaries than among us.

But it is evident that for a long time this also has been the public and most grievous complaint of all good men that Masses have been basely profaned and applied to purposes of lucre. For it is not unknown how far this abuse obtains in all the churches by what manner of men Masses are said only for fees or stipends, and how many celebrate them contrary to the Canons. But Paul severely threatens those who deal unworthily with the Eucharist when he says, 1 Cor.11,27: Whosoever shall eat this bread, and drink this cup of the Lord, unworthily, shall be guilty of the body and blood of the Lord. When, therefore our priests were admonished concerning this sin, Private Masses were discontinued among us, as scarcely any Private Masses were celebrated except for lucre's sake.

Neither were the bishops ignorant of these abuses, and if they had corrected them in time, there would now be less dissension. Heretofore, by their own connivance, they suffered many corruptions to creep into the Church. Now, when it is too late, they begin to complain of the troubles of the Church, while this disturbance has been occasioned simply by those abuses which were so manifest that they could be borne no longer. There have been great dissensions concerning the Mass, concerning the Sacrament. Perhaps the world is being punished for such long-continued profanations of the Mass as have been tolerated in the churches for so many centuries by the very men who were both able and in duty bound to correct them. For in the Ten Commandments it is written, Ex. 20, 7: The Lord will not hold him guiltless that taketh His name in vain. But since the world began, nothing that God ever ordained seems to have been so abused for filthy lucre as the Mass.

There was also added the opinion which infinitely increased Private Masses, namely that Christ, by His passion, had made satisfaction for original sin, and instituted the Mass wherein an offering should be made for daily sins, venial and mortal. From this has arisen the common opinion that the Mass takes away the sins of the living and the dead by the outward act. Then they began to dispute whether one Mass said for many were worth as much as special Masses for individuals, and this brought forth that infinite multitude of Masses. [With this work men wished to obtain from God all that they needed, and in the mean time faith in Christ and the true worship were forgotten.]

Concerning these opinions our teachers have given warning that they depart from the Holy Scriptures and diminish the glory of the passion of Christ. For Christ's passion was an oblation and satisfaction, not for original guilt only, but also for all other sins, as it is written to the Hebrews, 10, 10: We are sanctified through the offering of Jesus Christ once for all. Also, 10, 14: By one offering He hath perfected forever them that are sanctified. [It is an unheard-of innovation in the Church to teach that Christ by His death made satisfaction only for original sin and not likewise for all other sin. Accordingly it is hoped that everybody will understand that this error has not been reproved without due reason.]

Scripture also teaches that we are justified before God through faith in Christ, when we believe that our sins are forgiven for Christ's sake. Now if the Mass take away the sins of the living and the dead by the outward act justification comes of the work of Masses, and not of faith, which Scripture does not allow.

But Christ commands us, Luke 22, 19: This do in remembrance of Me; therefore the Mass was instituted that the faith of those who use the Sacrament should remember what benefits it receives through Christ, and cheer and comfort the anxious conscience. For to remember Christ is to remember His benefits, and to realize that they are truly offered unto us. Nor is it enough only to remember the history; for this also the Jews and the ungodly can remember. Wherefore the Mass is to be used to this end, that there the Sacrament [Communion] may be administered to them that have need of consolation; as Ambrose says: Because I always sin, I am always bound to take the medicine. [Therefore this Sacrament requires faith, and is used in vain without faith.]

Now, forasmuch as the Mass is such a giving of the Sacrament, we hold one communion every holy-day, and, if any desire the Sacrament, also on other days, when it is given to such as ask for it. And this custom is not new in the Church; for the Fathers before Gregory make no mention of any private Mass, but of the common Mass [the Communion] they speak very much. Chrysostom says that the priest stands daily at the altar, inviting some to the Communion and keeping back others. And it appears from the ancient Canons that some one celebrated the Mass from whom all the other presbyters and deacons received the body of the Lord; for thus the words of the Nicene Canon say: Let the deacons, according to their order, receive the Holy Communion after the presbyters, from the bishop or from a presbyter. And Paul, 1 Cor. 11, 33, commands concerning the Communion: Tarry one for another, so that there may be a common participation.

Forasmuch, therefore, as the Mass with us has the example of the Church, taken from the Scripture and the Fathers, we are confident that it cannot be disapproved, especially since public ceremonies, for the most part like those hitherto in use, are retained; only the number of Masses differs, which, because of very great and manifest abuses doubtless might be profitably reduced. For in olden times, even in churches most frequented, the Mass was not celebrated every day, as the Tripartite History (Book 9, chap. 33) testifies: Again in Alexandria, every Wednesday and Friday the Scriptures are read, and the doctors expound them, and all things are done, except the solemn rite of Communion.

ARTICLE XXV.

OF CONFESSION.

Confession in the churches is not abolished among us; for it is not usual to give the body of the Lord, except to them that have been previously examined and absolved. And the people are most carefully taught concerning faith in the absolution, about which formerly there was profound silence. Our people are taught that they should highly prize the absolution, as being the voice of God, and pronounced by God's command. The power of the Keys is set forth in its beauty and they are reminded what great consolation it brings to anxious consciences, also, that God requires faith to believe such absolution as a voice sounding from heaven, and that such faith in Christ truly obtains and receives the forgiveness of sins. Aforetime satisfactions were immoderately extolled; of faith and the merit of Christ and the righteousness of faith no mention was made; wherefore, on this point, our churches are by no means to be blamed. For this even our adversaries must needs concede to us that the doctrine concerning repentance has been most diligently treated and laid open by our teachers.

But of Confession they teach that an enumeration of sins is not necessary, and that consciences be not burdened with anxiety to enumerate all sins, for it is impossible to recount all sins, as the Psalm testifies, 19,13: Who can understand his errors? Also Jeremiah, 17 9: The heart is deceitful; who can know it; But if no sins were forgiven, except those that are recounted, consciences could never find peace; for very many sins they neither see nor can remember. The ancient writers also testify that an enumeration is not necessary. For in the Decrees, Chrysostom is quoted, who says thus: I say not to you that you should disclose yourself in public, nor that you accuse yourself before others, but I would have you obey the prophet who says: "Disclose thy self before God." Therefore confess your sins before God, the true Judge, with prayer. Tell your errors, not with the tongue, but with the memory of your conscience, etc. And the Gloss (Of Repentance, Distinct. V, Cap. Consideret) admits that Confession is of human right only [not commanded by Scripture, but ordained by the Church]. Nevertheless, on account of the great benefit of absolution, and because it is otherwise useful to the conscience, Confession is retained among us.

ARTICLE XXVI.

OF THE DISTINCTION OF MEATS.

It has been the general persuasion, not of the people alone, but also of those teaching in the churches, that making Distinctions of Meats, and like traditions of men, are works profitable to merit grace, and able to make satisfactions for sins. And that the world so thought, appears from this, that new ceremonies, new orders, new holy-days, and new fastings were daily instituted, and the teachers in the churches did exact these works as a service necessary to merit grace, and did greatly terrify men's consciences, if they should omit any of these things. From this persuasion concerning traditions much detriment has resulted in the Church.

First, the doctrine of grace and of the righteousness of faith has been obscured by it, which is the chief part of the Gospel, and ought to stand out as the most prominent in the Church, in order that the merit of Christ may be well known, and faith, which believes that sins are forgiven for Christ's sake be exalted far above works. Wherefore Paul also lays the greatest stress on this article, putting aside the Law and human traditions, in order to show that Christian righteousness is something else than such works, to wit, the faith which believes that sins are freely forgiven for Christ's sake. But this doctrine of Paul has been almost wholly smothered by traditions, which have produced an opinion that, by making distinctions in meats and like services, we must merit grace and righteousness. In treating of repentance, there was no mention made of faith; only those works of satisfaction were set forth; in these the entire repentance seemed to consist.

Secondly, these traditions have obscured the commandments of God, because traditions were placed far above the commandments of God. Christianity was thought to consist wholly in the observance of certain holy-days, rites, fasts, and vestures. These observances had won for themselves the exalted title of being the spiritual life and the perfect life. Meanwhile the commandments of God, according to each one's calling, were without honor namely, that the father brought up his offspring, that the mother bore children, that the prince governed the commonwealth,—these were accounted works that were worldly and imperfect, and far below those glittering observances. And this error greatly tormented devout consciences, which grieved that they were held in an imperfect state of life, as in marriage, in the office of magistrate; or in other civil ministrations; on the other hand, they admired the monks and such like, and falsely imagined that the observances of such men were more acceptable to God.

Thirdly, traditions brought great danger to consciences; for it was impossible to keep all traditions, and yet men judged these observances to be necessary acts of worship. Gerson writes that many fell into despair, and that some even took their own lives, because they felt that they were not able to satisfy the traditions, and they had all the while not heard any consolation of the righteousness of faith and grace. We see that the summists and theologians gather the traditions, and seek mitigations whereby to ease consciences, and yet they do not sufficiently unfetter, but sometimes entangle, consciences even more. And with the gathering of these traditions, the schools and sermons have been so much occupied that they have had no leisure to touch upon Scripture, and to seek the more profitable doctrine of faith, of the cross, of hope, of the dignity of civil affairs of consolation of sorely tried consciences. Hence Gerson and some other theologians have grievously complained that by these strivings concerning traditions they were prevented from giving attention to a better kind of doctrine. Augustine also forbids that men's consciences should be burdened with such observances, and prudently advises Januarius that he must know that they are to be observed as things indifferent; for such are his words.

Wherefore our teachers must not be looked upon as having taken up this matter rashly or from hatred of the bishops, as some falsely suspect. There was great need to warn the churches of these errors, which had arisen from misunderstanding the traditions. For the Gospel compels us to insist in the churches upon the doctrine of grace, and of the righteousness of faith; which, however, cannot be understood, if men think that they merit grace by observances of their own choice.

Thus, therefore, they have taught that by the observance of human traditions we cannot merit grace or be justified, and hence we must not think such observances necessary acts of worship. They add hereunto testimonies of Scripture. Christ, Matt. 15, 3, defends the Apostles who had not observed the usual tradition, which, however, evidently pertains to a matter not unlawful, but indifferent, and to have a certain affinity with the purifications of the Law, and says, 9: In vain do they worship Me with the commandments of men. He, therefore, does not exact an unprofitable service. Shortly after He adds: Not that which goeth into the mouth defileth a man. So also Paul, Rom. 14, 17: The kingdom of God is not meat and drink. Col. 2, 16: Let no man, therefore, judge you in meat, or in drink, or in respect of an holy-day, or of the Sabbath-day; also: If ye be dead with Christ from the rudiments of the world, why, as though living in the world, are ye subject to ordinances: Touch not, taste not, handle not! And Peter says, Acts 15, 10: Why tempt ye God to put a yoke upon the neck of the disciples, which neither our fathers nor we were able to bear? But we believe that through the grace of the Lord Jesus Christ we shall be saved, even as they. Here Peter forbids to burden the consciences with many rites, either of Moses or of others. And in 1 Tim. 4,1.3 Paul calls the prohibition of meats a doctrine of devils; for it is against the Gospel to institute or to do such works that by them we may merit grace, or as though Christianity could not exist without such service of God.

Here our adversaries object that our teachers are opposed to discipline and mortification of the flesh, as Jovinian. But the contrary may be learned from the writings of our teachers. For they have always taught concerning the cross that it behooves Christians to bear afflictions. This is the true, earnest, and unfeigned mortification, to wit, to be exercised with divers afflictions, and to be crucified with Christ.

Moreover, they teach that every Christian ought to train and subdue himself with bodily restraints, or bodily exercises and labors that neither satiety nor slothfulness tempt him to sin, but not that we may merit grace or make satisfaction for sins by such exercises. And such external discipline ought to be urged at all times, not only on a few and set days. So Christ commands, Luke 21, 34: Take heed lest your hearts be overcharged with surfeiting; also Matt. 17, 21: This kind goeth not out but by prayer and fasting. Paul also says, 1 Cor. 9, 27: I keep under my body and bring it into subjection. Here he clearly shows that he was keeping under his body, not to merit forgiveness of sins by that discipline, but to have his body in subjection and fitted for spiritual things, and for the discharge of duty according to his calling. Therefore, we do not condemn fasting in itself, but the traditions which prescribe certain days and certain meats, with peril of conscience, as though such works were a necessary service.

Nevertheless, very many traditions are kept on our part, which conduce to good order in the Church, as the Order of Lessons in the Mass and the chief holy-days. But, at the same time, men are warned that such observances do not justify before God, and that in such things it should not be made sin if they be omitted without offense. Such liberty in human rites was not unknown to the Fathers. For in the East they kept Easter at another time than at Rome, and when, on account of this diversity, the Romans accused the Eastern Church of schism, they were admonished by others that such usages need not be alike everywhere. And Irenaeus says: Diversity concerning fasting does not destroy the harmony of faith; as also Pope Gregory intimates in Dist. XII, that such diversity does not violate the unity of the Church. And in the Tripartite History, Book 9, many examples of dissimilar rites are gathered, and the following statement is made: It was not the mind of the Apostles to enact rules concerning holy-days, but to preach godliness and a holy life [, to teach faith and love].

ARTICLE XXVII.

OF MONASTIC VOWS.

What is taught on our part concerning Monastic Vows, will be better understood if it be remembered what has been the state of the monasteries, and how many things were daily done in those very monasteries, contrary to the Canons. In Augustine's time they were free associations. Afterward, when discipline was corrupted, vows were everywhere added for the purpose of restoring discipline, as in a carefully planned prison.

Gradually, many other observances were added besides vows. And these fetters were laid upon many before the lawful age, contrary to the Canons.

Many also entered into this kind of life through ignorance, being unable to judge their own strength, though they were of sufficient age. Being thus ensnared, they were compelled to remain, even though some could have been freed by the kind provision of the Canons. And this was more the case in convents of women than of monks, although more consideration should have been shown the weaker sex. This rigor displeased many good men before this time, who saw that young men and maidens were thrown into convents for a living. They saw what unfortunate results came of this procedure, and what scandals were created, what snares were cast upon consciences! They were grieved that the authority of the Canons in so momentous a matter was utterly set aside and despised. To these evils was added such a persuasion concerning vows as, it is well known, in former times displeased even those monks who were more considerate. They taught that vows were equal to Baptism; they taught that by this kind of life they merited forgiveness of sins and justification before God. Yea, they added that the monastic life not only merited righteousness before God but even greater things, because it kept not only the precepts, but also the so-called "evangelical counsels."

Thus they made men believe that the profession of monasticism was far better than Baptism, and that the monastic life was more meritorious than that of magistrates, than the life of pastors, and such like, who serve their calling in accordance with God's commands, without any man-made services. None of these things can be denied; for they appear in their own books. [Moreover, a person who has been thus ensnared and has entered a monastery learns little of Christ.]

What, then, came to pass in the monasteries? Aforetime they were schools of theology and other branches, profitable to the Church; and thence pastors and bishops were obtained. Now it is another thing. It is needless to rehearse what is known to all. Aforetime they came together to learn; now they feign that it is a kind of life instituted to merit grace and righteousness; yea, they preach that it is a state of perfection, and they put it far above all other kinds of life ordained of God. These things we have rehearsed without odious exaggeration, to the end that the doctrine of our teachers on this point might be better understood.

First, concerning such as contract matrimony, they teach on our part that it is lawful for all men who are not fitted for single life to contract matrimony, because vows cannot annul the ordinance and commandment of God. But the commandment of God is 1 Cor. 7, 2: To avoid fornication, let every man have his own wife. Nor is it the commandment only, but also the creation and ordinance of God, which forces those to marry who are not excepted by a singular work of God, according to the text Gen. 2, 18: It is not good that the man should be alone. Therefore they do not sin who obey this commandment and ordinance of God.

What objection can be raised to this? Let men extol the obligation of a vow as much as they list, yet shall they not bring to pass that the vow annuls the commandment of God. The Canons teach that the right of the superior is excepted in every vow; [that vows are not binding against the decision of the Pope;] much less, therefore, are these vows of force which are against the commandments of God.

Now, if the obligation of vows could not be changed for any cause whatever, the Roman Pontiffs could never have given dispensation for it is not lawful for man to annul an obligation which is simply divine. But the Roman Pontiffs have prudently judged that leniency is to be observed in this obligation, and therefore we read that many times they have dispensed from vows. The case of the King of Aragon who was called back from the monastery is well known, and there are also examples in our own times. [Now, if dispensations have been granted for the sake of securing temporal interests, it is much more proper that they be granted on account of the distress of souls.]

In the second place, why do our adversaries exaggerate the obligation or effect of a vow when, at the same time, they have not a word to say of the nature of the vow itself, that it ought to be in a thing possible, that it ought to be free, and chosen spontaneously and deliberately? But it is not unknown to what extent perpetual chastity is in the power of man. And how few are there who have taken the vow spontaneously and deliberately! Young maidens and men, before they are able to judge, are persuaded, and sometimes even compelled, to take the vow. Wherefore it is not fair to insist so rigorously on the obligation, since it is granted by all that it is against the nature of a vow to take it without spontaneous and deliberate action.

Most canonical laws rescind vows made before the age of fifteen; for before that age there does not seem sufficient judgment in a person to decide concerning a perpetual life. Another Canon, granting more to the weakness of man, adds a few years; for it forbids a vow to be made before the age of eighteen. But which of these two Canons shall we follow? The most part have an excuse for leaving the monasteries, because most of them have taken the vows before they reached these ages.

Finally, even though the violation of a vow might be censured, yet it seems not forthwith to follow that the marriages of such persons must be dissolved. For Augustine denies that they ought to be dissolved (XXVII. Quaest. I, Cap. Nuptiarum), and his authority is not lightly to be esteemed, although other men afterwards thought otherwise.

But although it appears that God's command concerning marriage delivers very many from their vows, yet our teachers introduce also another argument concerning vows to show that they are void. For every service of God, ordained and chosen of men without the commandment of God to merit justification and grace, is wicked, as Christ says Matt. 16, 9: In vain do they worship Me with the commandments of men. And Paul teaches everywhere that righteousness is not to be sought from our own observances and acts of worship, devised by men, but that it comes by faith to those who believe that they are received by God into grace for Christ's sake.

But it is evident that monks have taught that services of man's making satisfy for sins and merit grace and justification. What else is this than to detract from the glory of Christ and to obscure and deny the righteousness of faith? It follows, therefore, that the vows thus commonly taken have been wicked services, and, consequently, are void. For a wicked vow, taken against the commandment of God, is not valid; for (as the Canon says) no vow ought to bind men to wickedness.

Paul says, Gal. 5, 4: Christ is become of no effect unto you, whosoever of you are justified by the Law, ye are fallen from grace. To those, therefore, who want to be justified by their vows Christ is made of no effect, and they fall from grace. For also these who ascribe justification to vows ascribe to their own works that which properly belongs to the glory of Christ.

Nor can it be denied, indeed, that the monks have taught that, by their vows and observances, they were justified, and merited forgiveness of sins, yea, they invented still greater absurdities, saying that they could give others a share in their works. If any one should be inclined to enlarge on these things with evil intent, how many things could he bring together whereof even the monks are now ashamed! Over and above this, they persuaded men that services of man's making were a state of Christian perfection. And is not this assigning justification to works? It is no light offense in the Church to set forth to the people a service devised by men, without the commandment of God, and to teach that such service justifies men. For the righteousness of faith, which chiefly ought to be taught in the Church, is obscured when these wonderful angelic forms of worship, with their show of poverty, humility, and celibacy, are east before the eyes of men.

Furthermore, the precepts of God and the true service of God are obscured when men hear that only monks are in a state of perfection. For Christian perfection is to fear God from the heart, and yet to conceive great faith, and to trust that for Christ's sake we have a God who has been reconciled, to ask of God, and assuredly to expect His aid in all things that, according to our calling, are to be done; and meanwhile, to be diligent in outward good works, and to serve our calling. In these things consist the true perfection and the true service of God. It does not consist in celibacy, or in begging, or in vile apparel. But the people conceive many pernicious opinions from the false commendations of monastic life. They hear celibacy praised above measure; therefore they lead their married life with offense to their consciences. They hear that only beggars are perfect; therefore they keep their possessions and do business with offense to their consciences. They hear that it is an evangelical counsel not to seek revenge; therefore some in private life are not afraid to take revenge, for they hear that it is but a counsel, and not a commandment. Others judge that the Christian cannot properly hold a civil office or be a magistrate.

There are on record examples of men who, forsaking marriage and the administration of the Commonwealth, have hid themselves in monasteries. This they called fleeing from the world, and seeking a kind of life which would be more pleasing to God. Neither did they see that God ought to be served in those commandments which He Himself has given and not in commandments devised by men. A good and perfect kind of life is that which has for it the commandment of God. It is necessary to admonish men of these things.

And before these times, Gerson rebukes this error of the monks concerning perfection, and testifies that in his day it was a new saying that the monastic life is a state of perfection.

So many wicked opinions are inherent in the vows, namely, that they justify, that they constitute Christian perfection, that they keep the counsels and commandments, that they have works of supererogation. All these things, since they are false and empty, make vows null and void.

ARTICLE XXVIII.
OF ECCLESIASTICAL POWER.

There has been great controversy concerning the Power of Bishops, in which some have awkwardly confounded the power of the Church and the power of the sword. And from this confusion very great wars and tumults have resulted, while the Pontiffs, emboldened by the power of the Keys, not only have instituted new services and burdened consciences with reservation of cases and ruthless excommunications, but have also undertaken to transfer the kingdoms of this world, and to take the Empire from the Emperor. These wrongs have long since been rebuked in the Church by learned and godly men. Therefore our teachers, for the comforting of men's consciences, were constrained to show the difference between the power of the Church and the power of the sword, and taught that both of them, because of God's commandment, are to be held in reverence and honor, as the chief blessings of God on earth.

But this is their opinion, that the power of the Keys, or the power of the bishops, according to the Gospel, is a power or commandment of God, to preach the Gospel, to remit and retain sins, and to administer Sacraments. For with this commandment Christ sends forth His Apostles, John 20, 21 sqq.: As My Father hath sent Me, even so send I you. Receive ye the Holy Ghost. Whosesoever sins ye remit, they are remitted unto them; and whosesoever sins ye retain, they are retained. Mark 16, 15: Go preach the Gospel to every creature.

This power is exercised only by teaching or preaching the Gospel and administering the Sacraments, according to their calling either to many or to individuals. For thereby are granted, not bodily, but eternal things, as eternal righteousness, the Holy Ghost, eternal life. These things cannot come but by the ministry of the Word and the Sacraments, as Paul says, Rom. 1, 16: The Gospel is the power of God unto salvation to every one that believeth. Therefore, since the power of the Church grants eternal things, and is exercised only by the ministry of the Word, it does not interfere with civil government; no more than the art of singing interferes with civil government. For civil government deals with other things than does the Gospel. The civil rulers defend not minds, but bodies and bodily things against manifest injuries, and restrain men with the sword and bodily punishments in order to preserve civil justice and peace.

Therefore the power of the Church and the civil power must not be confounded. The power of the Church has its own commission to teach the Gospel and to administer the Sacraments. Let it not break into the office of another; Let it not transfer the kingdoms of this world; let it not abrogate the laws of civil rulers; let it not abolish lawful obedience; let it not interfere with judgments concerning civil ordinances or contracts; let it not prescribe laws to civil rulers concerning the form of the Commonwealth. As Christ says, John 18, 33: My kingdom is not of this world; also Luke 12, 14: Who made Me a judge or a divider over you? Paul also says, Phil. 3, 20: Our citizenship is in heaven; 2 Cor. 10, 4: The weapons of our warfare are not carnal, but mighty through God to the casting down of imaginations.

After this manner our teachers discriminate between the duties of both these powers, and command that both be honored and acknowledged as gifts and blessings of God. If bishops have any power of the sword, that power they have, not as bishops, by the commission of the Gospel, but by human law having received it of kings and emperors for the civil administration of what is theirs. This, however, is another office than the ministry of the Gospel.

When, therefore, the question is concerning the jurisdiction of bishops, civil authority must be distinguished from ecclesiastical jurisdiction. Again, according to the Gospel or, as they say, by divine right, there belongs to the bishops as bishops, that is, to those to whom has been committed the ministry of the Word and the Sacraments, no jurisdiction except to forgive sins, to judge doctrine, to reject doctrines contrary to the Gospel, and to exclude from the communion of the Church wicked men, whose wickedness is known, and this without human force, simply by the Word. Herein the congregations of necessity and by divine right must obey them, according to Luke 10, 16: He that heareth you heareth Me. But when they teach or ordain anything against the Gospel, then the congregations have a commandment of God prohibiting obedience, Matt. 7, 15: Beware of false prophets; Gal. 1, 8: Though an angel from heaven preach any other gospel, let him be accursed; 2 Cor. 13, 8: We can do nothing against the truth, but for the truth. Also: The power which the Lord hath given me to edification, and not to destruction. So, also, the Canonical Laws command (II. Q. VII. Cap., Sacerdotes, and Cap. Oves). And Augustine (Contra Petiliani Epistolam): Neither must we submit to Catholic bishops if they chance to err, or hold anything contrary to the Canonical Scriptures of God.

If they have any other power or jurisdiction, in hearing and judging certain cases, as of matrimony or of tithes, etc., they have it by human right, in which matters princes are bound, even against their will, when the ordinaries fail, to dispense justice to their subjects for the maintenance of peace.

Moreover, it is disputed whether bishops or pastors have the right to introduce ceremonies in the Church, and to make laws concerning meats, holy-days and grades, that is, orders of ministers, etc. They that give this right to the bishops refer to this testimony John 16, 12. 13: I have yet many things to say unto you, but ye cannot bear them now. Howbeit when He, the Spirit of Truth, is come, He will guide you into all truth. They also refer to the example of the Apostles, who commanded to abstain from blood and from things strangled, Acts 15, 29. They refer to the Sabbath-day as having been changed into the Lord's Day, contrary to the Decalog, as it seems. Neither is there any example whereof they make more than concerning the changing of the Sabbath-day. Great, say they, is the power of the

Church, since it has dispensed with one of the Ten Commandments!

But concerning this question it is taught on our part (as has been shown above) that bishops have no power to decree anything against the Gospel. The Canonical Laws teach the same thing (Dist. IX). Now, it is against Scripture to establish or require the observance of any traditions, to the end that by such observance we may make satisfaction for sins, or merit grace and righteousness. For the glory of Christ's merit suffers injury when, by such observances, we undertake to merit justification. But it is manifest that, by such belief, traditions have almost infinitely multiplied in the Church, the doctrine concerning faith and the righteousness of faith being meanwhile suppressed. For gradually more holy-days were made, fasts appointed, new ceremonies and services in honor of saints instituted, because the authors of such things thought that by these works they were meriting grace. Thus in times past the Penitential Canons increased, whereof we still see some traces in the satisfactions.

Again, the authors of traditions do contrary to the command of God when they find matters of sin in foods, in days, and like things, and burden the Church with bondage of the law, as if there ought to be among Christians, in order to merit justification a service like the Levitical, the arrangement of which God had committed to the Apostles and bishops. For thus some of them write; and the Pontiffs in some measure seem to be misled by the example of the law of Moses. Hence are such burdens, as that they make it mortal sin, even without offense to others, to do manual labor on holy-days, a mortal sin to omit the Canonical Hours, that certain foods defile the conscience that fastings are works which appease God that sin in a reserved case cannot be forgiven but by the authority of him who reserved it; whereas the Canons themselves speak only of the reserving of the ecclesiastical penalty, and not of the reserving of the guilt.

Whence have the bishops the right to lay these traditions upon the Church for the ensnaring of consciences, when Peter, Acts 15, 10, forbids to put a yoke upon the neck of the disciples, and Paul says, 2 Cor. 13, 10, that the power given him was to edification not to destruction? Why, therefore, do they increase sins by these traditions?

But there are clear testimonies which prohibit the making of such traditions, as though they merited grace or were necessary to salvation. Paul says, Col. 2, 16-23: Let no man judge you in meat, or in drink, or in respect of an holy-day, or of the new moon, or of the Sabbath-days. If ye be dead with Christ from the rudiments of the world, why, as though living in the world, are ye subject to ordinances (touch not; taste not; handle not, which all are to perish with the using) after the commandments and doctrines of men! which things have indeed a show of wisdom. Also in Titus 1, 14 he openly forbids traditions: Not giving heed to Jewish fables and commandments of men that turn from the truth.

And Christ, Matt. 15, 14. 13, says of those who require traditions: Let them alone; they be blind leaders of the blind; and He rejects such services: Every plant which My heavenly Father hath not planted shall be plucked up.

If bishops have the right to burden churches with infinite traditions, and to ensnare consciences, why does Scripture so often prohibit to make, and to listen to, traditions? Why does it call them "doctrines of devils"? 1 Tim. 4, 1. Did the Holy Ghost in vain forewarn of these things?

Since, therefore, ordinances instituted as things necessary, or with an opinion of meriting grace, are contrary to the Gospel, it follows that it is not lawful for any bishop to institute or exact such services. For it is necessary that the doctrine of Christian liberty be preserved in the churches, namely, that the bondage of the Law is not necessary to justification, as it is written in the Epistle to the Galatians, 5, 1: Be not entangled again with the yoke of bondage. It is necessary that the chief article of the Gospel be preserved, to wit, that we obtain grace freely by faith in Christ, and not for certain observances or acts of worship devised by men.

What, then, are we to think of the Sunday and like rites in the house of God? To this we answer that it is lawful for bishops or pastors to make ordinances that things be done orderly in the Church, not that thereby we should merit grace or make satisfaction for sins, or that consciences be bound to judge them necessary services, and to think that it is a sin to break them without offense to others. So Paul ordains, 1 Cor. 11, 5, that women should cover their heads in the congregation, 1 Cor. 14, 30, that interpreters be heard in order in the church, etc.

It is proper that the churches should keep such ordinances for the sake of love and tranquillity, so far that one do not offend another, that all things be done in the churches in order, and without confusion, 1 Cor. 14, 40; comp. Phil. 2, 14; but so that consciences be not burdened to think that they are necessary to salvation, or to judge that they sin when they break them without offense to others; as no one will say that a woman sins who goes out in public with her head uncovered provided only that no offense be given.

Of this kind is the observance of the Lord's Day, Easter, Pentecost, and like holy-days and rites. For those who judge that by the authority of the Church the observance of the Lord's Day instead of the Sabbath-day was ordained as a thing necessary, do greatly err. Scripture has abrogated the Sabbath-day; for it teaches that, since the Gospel has been revealed, all the ceremonies of Moses can be omitted. And yet, because it was necessary to appoint a certain day, that the people might know when they ought to come together, it appears that the Church designated the Lord's Day for this purpose; and this day seems to have been chosen all the more for this additional reason, that men might have an example of Christian liberty, and might know that the keeping neither of the Sabbath nor of any other day is necessary. There are monstrous disputations concerning the changing of the law, the ceremonies of the new law, the changing of the Sabbath-day, which all have sprung from the false belief that there must needs be in the Church a service like to the Levitical, and that Christ had given commission to the Apostles and bishops to devise new ceremonies as necessary to salvation. These errors crept into the Church when the righteousness of faith was not taught clearly enough. Some dispute that the keeping of the Lord's Day is not indeed of divine right, but in a manner so. They prescribe concerning holy-days, how far it is lawful to work. What else are such disputations than snares of consciences? For although they endeavor to modify the traditions, yet the mitigation can never be perceived as long as the opinion remains that they are necessary, which must needs remain where the righteousness of faith and Christian liberty are not known.

The Apostles commanded Acts 15, 20 to abstain from blood. Who does now observe it? And yet they that do it not sin not; for not even the Apostles themselves wanted to burden consciences with such bondage; but they forbade it for a time, to avoid offense. For in this decree we must perpetually consider what the aim of the Gospel is.

Scarcely any Canons are kept with exactness, and from day to day many go out of use even among those who are the most zealous advocates of traditions. Neither can due regard be paid to consciences unless this mitigation be observed, that we know that the Canons are kept without holding them to be necessary, and that no harm is done consciences, even though traditions go out of use.

But the bishops might easily retain the lawful obedience of the people if they would not insist upon the observance of such traditions as cannot be kept with a good conscience. Now they command celibacy; they admit none unless they swear that they will not teach the pure doctrine of the Gospel. The churches do not ask that the bishops should restore concord at the expense of their honor; which, nevertheless, it would be proper for good pastors to do. They ask only that they would release unjust burdens which are new and have been received contrary to the custom of the Church Catholic. It may be that in the beginning there were plausible reasons for some of these ordinances; and yet they are not adapted to later times. It is also evident that some were adopted through erroneous conceptions. Therefore it would be befitting the clemency of the Pontiffs to mitigate them now, because such a modification does not shake the unity of the Church. For many human traditions have been changed in process of time, as the Canons themselves show. But if it be impossible to obtain a mitigation of such observances as cannot be kept without sin, we are bound to follow the apostolic rule, Acts 5, 29, which commands us to obey God rather than men.

Peter, 1 Pet. 5, 3, forbids bishops to be lords, and to rule over the churches. It is not our design now to wrest the government from the bishops, but this one thing is asked, namely, that they allow the Gospel to be purely taught, and that they relax some few observances which cannot be kept without sin. But if they make no concession, it is for them to see how they shall give account to God for furnishing, by their obstinacy, a cause for schism.

CONCLUSION.

These are the chief articles which seem to be in controversy. For although we might have spoken of more abuses, yet, to avoid undue length, we have set forth the chief points, from which the rest may be readily judged. There have been great complaints concerning indulgences, pilgrimages, and the abuse of excommunications. The parishes have been vexed in many ways by the dealers in indulgences. There were endless contentions between the pastors and the monks concerning the parochial right, confessions, burials, sermons on extraordinary occasions, and innumerable other things. Issues of this sort we have passed over so that the chief points in this matter, having been briefly set forth, might be the more readily understood. Nor has anything been here said or adduced to the reproach of any one. Only those things have been recounted whereof we thought that it was necessary to speak, in order that it might be understood that in doctrine and ceremonies nothing has been received on our part against Scripture or the Church Catholic. For it is manifest that we have taken most diligent care that no new and ungodly doctrine should creep into our churches.

The above articles we desire to present in accordance with the edict of Your Imperial Majesty, in order to exhibit our Confession and let men see a summary of the doctrine of our teachers. If there is anything that any one might desire in this Confession, we are ready, God willing, to present ampler information according to the Scriptures.

Your Imperial Majesty's faithful subjects:

John, Duke of Saxony, Elector.
George, Margrave of Brandenburg.
Ernest, Duke of Lueneberg.
Philip, Landgrave of Hesse.
John Frederick, Duke of Saxony.
Francis, Duke of Lueneburg.
Wolfgang, Prince of Anhalt.
Senate and Magistracy of Nuremburg.
Senate of Reutlingen.

Lector House believes that a society develops through a two-fold approach of continuous learning and adaptation, which is derived from the study of classic literary works spread across the historic timeline of literature records. Therefore, we aim at reviving, repairing and redeveloping all those inaccessible or damaged but historically as well as culturally important literature across subjects so that the future generations may have an opportunity to study and learn from past works to embark upon a journey of creating a better future.

This book is a result of an effort made by Lector House towards making a contribution to the preservation and repair of original ancient works which might hold historical significance to the approach of continuous learning across subjects.

HAPPY READING & LEARNING!

LECTOR HOUSE LLP
E-MAIL: lectorpublishing@gmail.com